Oxford International Resources

7

Skills

Financial Literacy

Rotimi Merriman-Johnson

OXFORD UNIVERSITY PRESS

OXFORD
UNIVERSITY PRESS

Great Clarendon Street, Oxford, OX2 6DP, United Kingdom

Oxford University Press is a department of the University of Oxford. It furthers the University's objective of excellence in research, scholarship, and education by publishing worldwide. Oxford is a registered trade mark of Oxford University Press in the UK and in certain other countries.

First published in 2025

British Library Cataloguing in Publication Data
Data available

978-1-382-04559-9

10 9 8 7 6 5 4 3 2 1

The manufacturing process conforms to the environmental regulations of the country of origin.

Printed in China by Golden Cup

The manufacturer's authorised representative in the EU for product safety is Oxford University Press España S.A. of el Parque Empresarial San Fernando de Henares, Avenida de Castilla, 2 – 28830 Madrid (www.oup.es/en or product.safety@oup.com). OUP España S.A. also acts as importer into Spain of products made by the manufacturer.

Acknowledgements

Written by Rotimi Merriman-Johnson

The publisher and authors would like to thank the following for permission to use photographs and other copyright material:

Cover: Florimond Mochel. **Photos: p5:** baja / Shutterstock; **p7:** VAKS-Stock Agency / Shutterstock; **p8:** Jason M. Fong / Shutterstock; **p9:** Monkey Business Images / Shutterstock; **p10(tm):** WBMUL / Shutterstock; **p10(bm):** koonsiri boonnak / Shutterstock; **p10(tl):** Ground Picture / Shutterstock; **p10(tr):** Billion Photos / Shutterstock; **p10(bl):** Pressmaster / Shutterstock; **p10(br):** Wit Olszewski / Shutterstock; **p11(t):** Zamrznuti tonovi / Shutterstock; **p11(b):** cobalt88 / Shutterstock; **p14:** szefei / Shutterstock; **p17:** abdrahimmahfar / Shutterstock; **p18:** ldutko / Shutterstock; **p20(t):** Ikiry GR / Shutterstock; **p20(b):** Yelena Panyukova / Shutterstock; **p21:** DedMityay / Shutterstock; **p22(l):** oneinchpunch / Shutterstock; **p22(m):** fizkes / Shutterstock; **p22(r):** Trendsetter Images / Shutterstock; **p23(t):** stockpexel / Shutterstock; **p23(b):** Roman Kosolapov / Shutterstock; **p24(t):** vnlit / Shutterstock / Shutterstock; **p24(b):** KucherAV / Shutterstock; **p28:** Pakhnyushchy / Shutterstock; **p29:** Olga Yemets / Shutterstock; **p30:** Sebastian Duda / Shutterstock; **p32(t):** namtipStudio / Shutterstock; **p32(b):** Natalia Deriabina / Shutterstock; **p33:** ASDF_MEDIA / Shutterstock; **p34(A):** Loveshop / Shutterstock; **p34(B):** Globe Turner / Shutterstock; **p34(C):** PVLGT / Shutterstock; **p34(D):** Maximumvector / Shutterstock; **p34(E):** nortongo / Shutterstock; **p34(F):** Peter Probst / Shutterstock; **p35(t):** Nalidsa / Shutterstock; **p35(b):** Hadrian / Shutterstock; **p36(t):** Rawpixel.com / Shutterstock; **p36(b):** Rawpixel.com / Shutterstock; **p38:** jijomathaidesigners / Shutterstock; **p39:** Bird stocker TH / Shutterstock; **p41:** Nana_studio / Shutterstock; **p42:** Roman Samborskyi / Shutterstock; **p43:** Ground Picture / Shutterstock; **p44:** Dean Drobot / Shutterstock; **p45:** Yuriy K / Shutterstock; **p46:** Andy Dean Photography / Shutterstock; **p47(t):** grinny / Shutterstock; **p47(b):** Dmitry Kalinovsky / Shutterstock; **p48:** Ground Picture / Shutterstock; **p49:** vivat / Shutterstock; **p50:** rnl / Shutterstock; **p52:** Ground Picture / Shutterstock; **p53:** NazArt / Shutterstock; **p55:** Andrey_Popov / Shutterstock; **p57:** IM_photo / Shutterstock; **p58(t):** Stefan Balaz / Shutterstock; **p58(b):** ClassicVector / Shutterstock; **p59:** Issarawat Tattong / Shutterstock; **p60(l):** vasabii / Shutterstock; **p60(m):** Vtls / Shutterstock; **p60(r):** KsanderDN / Shutterstock; **p61:** Ken Gamage / Oxford University Press; **p62(t):** iofoto / Shutterstock; **p62(b):** BearFotos / Shutterstock; **p63(A):** Karkas / Shutterstock; **p63(B):** Dennis Kitchen Studio, Inc / Oxford University Press; **p63(C):** conzorb / Shutterstock; **p63(D):** Lilkin / Shutterstock; **p64:** Grigvovan / Shutterstock; **p65:** CeltStudio / Shutterstock; **p68:** Tero Vesalainen / Shutterstock; **p69:** PeopleImages.com - Yuri A / Shutterstock; **p71:** INDz / Shutterstock; **p72:** MargJohnsonVA / Shutterstock; **p73:** Jack_the_sparow / Shutterstock; **p75:** Alex Staroseltsev / Shutterstock.

Artwork by QBS Learning, Daniel Limon, Anthony Rule, Peter Stevenson, Emma Trithart, Peppy Design Works, Andy Hamilton, Eva Sassin, Judy Brown, Mark Ruffle, Michael Emmerson, Mircea Catusanu, Robin Davies, The Flag Institute, and Oxford University Press.

Contents

1 Getting started with money

Talking to adults about money

You can learn about money by talking to adults in your family.

You can speak to adults in your family about how money works, or you can ask them for advice about your personal financial situation.

If you have never spoken to any adults in your family about money before, here are some examples of questions to ask.

1 **a** What other questions could you ask adults in your family about money?

Write your questions here:

....

....

....

....

b With a partner, discuss whether you think each other's questions are appropriate or not and why.

You can also learn about money from your teachers.

Teachers are there to talk to you about how money works, not about your personal financial situation.

For example, you could ask your teachers about **mortgages**, **debit cards**, **budgets**, or **savings accounts**.

2 **a** Do you know the meanings of these terms? Draw a line to match each term to its description.

Term	Definition
mortgage	a standard **bank account**
debit card	a way of protecting something you own against an accident or loss
budget	a **loan** taken out to buy a property
savings account	equipment used to pay for things without using cash
checking account	a place to keep your money for a later date
insurance	a way of tracking and planning your spending

b Write a list of any other financial terms you have heard that you would like to talk to your teacher about.

____

____

Sometimes you might need to interact with adults you do not know about money. For example, store clerks and restaurant waiting staff.

You must never feel pressured to give information you are not comfortable with giving. Always speak to a trusted adult in your family if you are unsure.

3 In which location might you hear each of the following common phrases?

Write the possible location(s) next to each question.

Would you like the **bill**? ______________________________

How would you like to pay, cash or card? ______________________________

How much money would you like to **deposit**? ______________________________

Please insert your card into the **chip and pin device**. ______________________________

Do you need any insurance on this package? ______________________________

Talking to friends about money

As you get older, you will talk to your friends about money more and more.

1 **a** Write an appropriate response to each of the following questions a friend might ask you about money.

b Compare your answers with a partner's answers.

For each question, discuss whose answer is the most useful.

Sometimes you and your friends might pay for something together. For example, a meal in a restaurant, a video game or a birthday present for another one of your friends.

2 One Saturday morning, Billy and his six friends go for breakfast together at a café. The total bill is $45.50. Billy and his friends each pay an equal share of the bill. After breakfast, two of the friends go home. In the afternoon, Billy and the four remaining friends together buy a birthday present for another friend. The present costs $40.25. Billy and his four friends each pay an equal share of the cost. Later that day, Billy and one of his friends buy a video game together. The game costs $55.40 and they each pay half of the cost.

How much did Billy spend, in total, that day?

Show your working.

You might sometimes **lend** money to family members or friends. If you lend money, it is best to be cautious. If the person does not **repay** the money, it might result in disagreements.

3 Billy's sister Pam lends him $87.90. Billy agrees to repay the money in equal **instalments** of $15 a month.

a After how many months will Billy have repaid all of the money?

b How much **change** will Pam need to give Billy from his final instalment?

How people from different cultures talk about money

People from different cultures have different customs related to money. In some countries, it is customary for diners to give a **tip** to the waiting staff at a restaurant or to give the driver a tip after a taxi ride. In other countries, it is customary to give money to a place of worship or to the local community.

In China, during Lunar New Year, it is customary to give children gifts of red envelopes filled with notes or coins. These envelopes represent good wishes and good luck for the year ahead.

1 **a** Can you think of any examples of customs related to money where you live? Discuss with a partner.

b Do you know of any other customs related to money from other cultures? Discuss with a partner.

The history of money can be traced back to 6000 years ago. As a result, most languages around the world have a word for 'money'.

2 **a** Draw lines to match the words for 'money' on the left to the languages that they come from on the right.

Dinero	Japanese
Деньги (Dengi)	Russian
钱 (Qián)	Spanish
نقود (Naqud)	Mandarin Chinese
Argent	Portuguese
पैसे (Paise)	Swahili
Pesa	German
Geld	Hindi
お金 (Okane)	Arabic
Dinheiro	French

b Do you know the word for 'money' in any other language?

Write the words and the languages they are from.

The amount of money given as a tip is often calculated as a percentage of the total cost/**fee** of the service provided. This percentage often depends on the country and also on the service provided.

3 **a** Is it customary to give a tip for specific **services** where you live?

If yes, do you know how much people usually give as a tip?

Is the amount given as a tip different for different services?

Discuss with a partner.

b Mr Jackson and his family take a taxi ride from their home to the airport. The trip costs $160 in total. The taxi driver expects a tip of 15%. What is the total cost of the journey with the tip included?

In some cultures, it is customary to donate money to charities. People might donate money **weekly**, **monthly**, or **annually**.

4 Mr Jackson earns $50 000 a year. He donates 10% of his **gross salary** every week to the local food donation centre. In one particular year, Mr Jackson missed three weeks of donations. How much did he donate, in total, that year, to the nearest cent?

How money has changed throughout history

Money has taken several different forms throughout history, from coins and notes, to cheques and debit cards, and to cryptocurrency in 2009.

1 Write the name of the payment method shown in each image.

The first official **cheque** was created by the Bank of England in 1830. You might have seen oversized cheques given to the winners on TV game shows.

A cheque usually shows the amount of money to be paid in both numerals and words.

2 Write, in words, each amount of money below.

a $27 385 649 ______________________

b $5 734 821 ______________________

c $68 921 537 ______________________

d $14 963 240 ______________________

e $82 409 176 ______________________

f $3 271 908 ______________________

Coins were first invented over 2000 years ago. Coins and notes are some of the earliest forms of money. Debit cards were invented much more recently, in the 1960s.

An **ATM**, also invented in the 1960s, enables customers to **withdraw** physical money using a debit card.

Many ATMs are free to use. However, some ATMs charge customers a fee to withdraw money.

3 While on holiday in Sri Lanka, Nancy made the following **withdrawals**:

- 4 ATM withdrawals at a fee of 930 Sri Lankan Rupees per withdrawal
- 2 ATM withdrawals at a fee of 855 Sri Lankan Rupees per withdrawal
- 5 ATM withdrawals at a fee of 1305 Sri Lankan Rupees per withdrawal

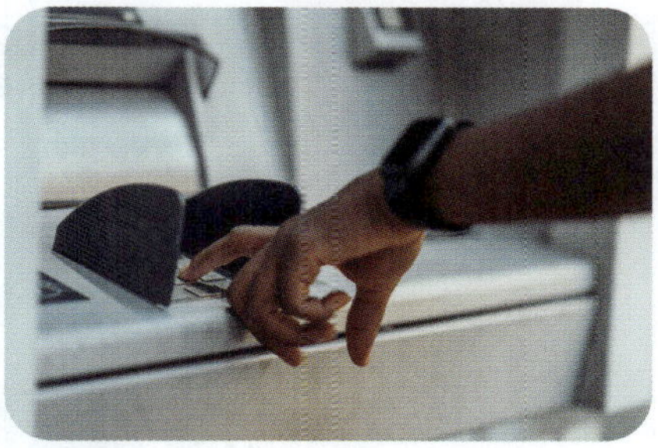

How much did Nancy pay in ATM fees, in total, during her holiday?

Give your answer in Sri Lankan Rupees.

Today, many people use their phones, and even sometimes their smartwatches, to make payments. These are called **mobile payments**. Mobile payments were first created at the start of the 2000s.

4 Jian is on holiday with his mother, father, sister and brother.

Jian's father uses his mobile payment app to buy some snacks for Jian, his sister and brother. He buys three packets of crisps that cost $1.20 each, two bottles of juice that cost $0.80 each and a bottle of water that costs $0.40. He has $10 in his **mobile wallet**.

a How much money does Jian's father have left in his mobile wallet after buying the snacks?

b Does Jian's father have enough money in his mobile wallet to also pay for three chocolate bars that cost $1.50 each?

Money at the supermarket

1 Khalid lives in Saudi Arabia. The currency in Saudi Arabia is the Saudi Riyal (SAR).

Khalid goes to the supermarket to buy some groceries.

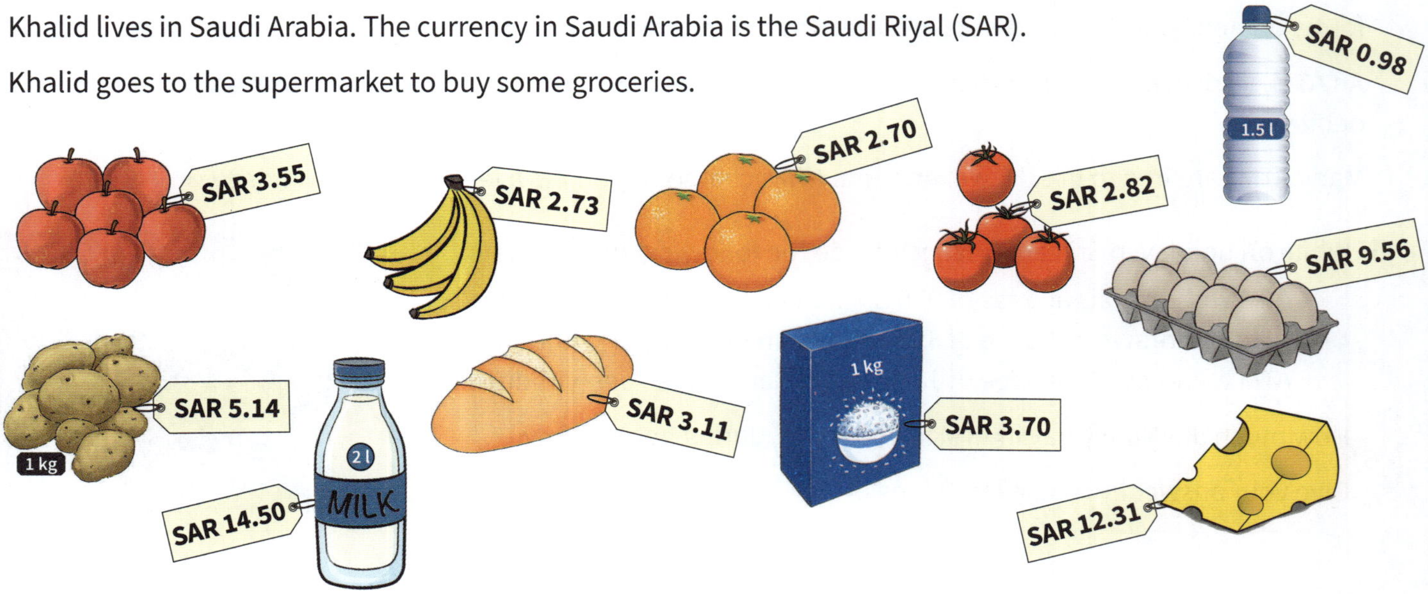

How much does Khalid spend to buy:

a six apples and a block of cheese

b eight tomatoes, a bunch of bananas and a box of eggs

c 1 kg of rice and 4.5 litres of water

d one of every item listed above?

2 Khalid also needs to buy some cashew nuts and some lentils. The supermarket sells cashew nuts and lentils in three different sized packages.

a Which size package of cashew nuts is the best **value for money**?

b Which size package of lentils is the best value for money?

Explain your reasoning.

c Buying in **bulk** is often better value for money. However, can you think of any disadvantages of buying perishable items in bulk?

Discuss with a partner.

If something is perishable, it is likely to decay or go bad quickly.

3 Khalid returns to the same supermarket the next week. There are **discounts** on some of the fruit and vegetables.

Work out the price of each item after the discount is applied to the original price. Where appropriate, round your answers to two decimal places.

a 20% off 6 apples

b 45% off a bunch of bananas

c 15% off 4 oranges

d 30% off 4 tomatoes

Simple money calculations

A person's **disposable income** is how much money they have left after subtracting their bills and **expenses** from their **income**.

1 Bian's income is $1000 per month. At the beginning of the month, the following expenses are automatically deducted from her bank account.

rent ($300)

groceries ($150)

utilities ($100)

transportation costs ($50)

phone bill ($30)

internet bill ($20)

savings ($100)

entertainment subscription ($15)

a What is Bian's disposable income for the month?

b Which of the above expenses do you think are **essential** and which of the expenses are **non-essential**?

Write each expense in the appropriate column.

Essential	Non-essential

Essential expenses are things you have to pay for. Non-essential expenses are things which are nice to have, but you can stop paying for if needed.

Compare your lists with a partner and discuss any differences.

Sometimes, you can use multiplication when calculating with money. For example, when working out how much money someone earns in one week, one month or one year.

2 Oliver earns $12.25 per hour for his job. He works 8 hours a day for 5 days a week. How much does Oliver earn in:

a one day

b one week

c one year?

Division is also an important maths skill to use when calculating with money. You will need to use division when budgeting, making payments and saving.

3 Zara receives $100 per month as her **allowance**. She wants to save money to buy a new bicycle. The bicycle costs $400.

Zara decides to save half of her allowance each month.

How many months will it take for Zara to save enough money to buy the bicycle?

2 Budgeting

The 50/30/20 principle

You can use the **50/30/20 principle** to **budget** your money.

As a guideline, the principle says that when you earn money you should spend 50% of the money on your 'needs', you should spend 30% of the money on your 'wants' and you should save 20% of the money.

1 **a** What is the difference between a 'need' and a 'want'?

Discuss with a partner.

b Below are ten example expenses. Put a tick in each row to show whether you think each expense is a need, a want or a saving.

For some of the expenses, there is no 'right' answer.

Compare your table with a partner's table and discuss your reasoning.

	Need	Want	Saving
Keeping money in a money box			
Buying groceries from the supermarket			
Buying clothes for school			
Going to the cinema			
Giving money to charity			
Buying a birthday present for a friend			
Buying a new phone			
Buying a new pair of sneakers			
Paying money into a savings account			
Setting aside your pocket money			

2 Below are five monthly income amounts. For each income amount, use the 50/30/20 principle to calculate how much money to spend on needs, how much money to spend on wants and how much money to save.

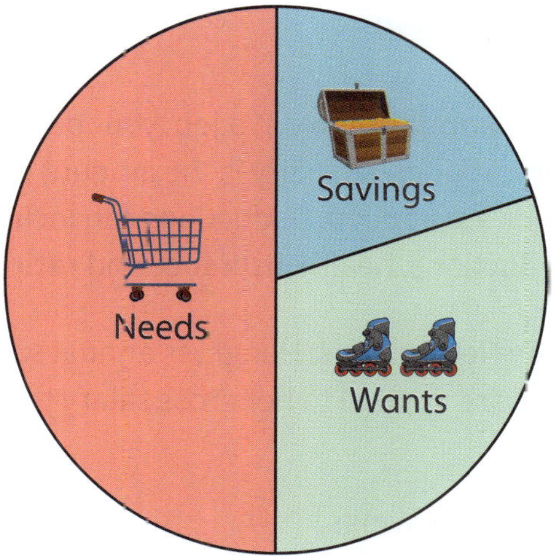

	Needs (50%)	Wants (30%)	Savings (20%)
$2300			
$1800			
$3450			
$2550			
$1340			

3 **a** Below are five different amounts of money that have been *saved* using the 50/30/20 principle.

Use this principle to calculate the original total amounts earned for each of the amounts saved.

i $40

ii $500

iii $760

iv $120

If you know 20% of a number, you can use division and multiplication to find the whole (100%).

First divide the 20% value by 2 to get 10% of the whole. Then multiply by 10 to get 100% (the whole amount).

b What type of things might people save money for? Discuss with a partner.

Calculating income

When you earn an **annual salary** in a job, your pay is usually expressed as your gross **salary**. Your gross salary is the amount of money you are paid, before deductions are applied. Deductions can include, for example, taxes, student loan deductions, health insurance and **retirement savings**.

1 Sofie lives in the Netherlands. Her gross annual salary is €24 000. The annual deductions that are applied to her gross salary to determine her **net pay** are:

€3000 for taxes

€1200 for retirement savings

€600 for health insurance

€900 for transportation costs

How much is Sofie's net pay, <u>each month</u>, after these deductions are applied?

Some jobs pay 'by the hour'. To calculate how much money you earn in a month, you need to calculate the number of hours worked that month, and then multiply this number by the **hourly rate**. The hourly rate might be higher on days such as weekends or public holidays or if you work **overtime**.

2 Deon works part-time at a local clothes store. He is paid by the hour. His hourly rate is $13.50.

Last month, Deon worked 16 hours in week one, 8 hours in week two, 24 hours in week three and 4 hours in week four.

6 of the hours he worked were overtime. For overtime hours he was paid double the usual hourly rate.

a How much was Deon paid last month?

b How much would Deon be paid for working the same hours if he was paid triple the usual rate for overtime hours?

Sometimes, people have multiple jobs to increase their total income. For example, they might have a weekday job and then a job they work on the weekends, or they might have a **freelance** job as well as their main job.

3 Alex has three jobs. He is a teacher, a freelance artist and a part-time tutor. He earns money from all three of these jobs.

From his teaching job, Alex earns \$3000 a month. From his freelance artist work, Alex earns \$50 per week. From tutoring, Alex earns \$15 per hour. He tutors for 8 hours each weekend.

Calculate Alex's total monthly earnings from all three jobs. You may assume that there are four weeks in a month.

When a person receives a **promotion**, they also usually receive a **pay rise**.

A pay rise can be expressed as a total amount or as a percentage.

4 A person earning \$30 000 receives a promotion and a 10% pay rise.

a By how much will their annual salary increase?

\$

b What will their total annual salary be after their pay rise?

\$

c By how much will their monthly salary increase?

\$

d What will their total monthly salary be after their pay rise?

\$

Calculating expenses

Some expenses to be paid out of a monthly budget are fixed. These expenses are the same amount each month. For example, rent, bills and subscriptions.

1 Samira pays several bills out of her monthly budget. Every month, she spends $750 on rent, $50 on electricity, $30 on gas, $40 on water, and $20 on internet.

Calculate how much Samira spends in a year on these **fixed expenses**.

Some expenses are variable. **Variable expenses** change from month to month.

2 As well as her fixed monthly expenses, Samira spends a variable amount on groceries each month. She recorded how much she spent on groceries each month last year, as shown below. She did not record a value for August.

Month	Amount spent on groceries
January	$80
February	$70
March	$90
April	$100
May	$85
June	$95
July	$75
August	?
September	$90
October	$100
November	$95
December	$110

a Samira spent $1085, in total, on groceries last year. How much did she spend on groceries in August?

$ ☐

b Samira would like to know her average monthly spend on groceries last year. Calculate the mean monthly amount she spent on groceries, rounded to the nearest cent.

$$\text{mean} = \frac{\text{sum of values}}{\text{number of values}}$$

$ ☐

Categorizing expenses helps you to identify trends in your spending. It also helps you to identify where you could make changes to spend more or less on different categories.

3 Mario has a monthly net income of $1842. His expenses for one month are categorized in the table.

Rent	Groceries	Bills	Transportation	Entertainment

$300	$200	$100	$150	$50

a Calculate how much Mario spent on each category as a percentage of his monthly income. Round each category to the nearest percent.

Rent ....

Groceries ....

Bills ....

Transportation ....

Entertainment ....

b How much money does Mario have left over, as a percentage of his monthly income. Round to the nearest percent.

☐ %

4 Leila earns $1246 per month. Last month, Leila spent $400 on rent, $250 on groceries, $150 on utilities, $150 on transportation, $50 on entertainment, $100 on dining out and $50 on clothing.

Leila would like to save $200 per month.

Which expenses do you think she could reduce to achieve her savings target? Discuss with a partner.

Calculating disposable income

Income is money that we earn or that is given to us. For example, earnings from a job, pocket money or birthday money.

An expense is something that we use money to pay for. Expenses can be 'needs' or they can be 'wants'.

Disposable income is the amount of money you have left after you spend money on your 'needs' and put aside any savings. 'Needs' include fixed expenses, for example, rent, bills and essential transport.

You use your disposable income to live and to pay for your 'wants', for example, holidays and leisure activities.

1 Look at the monthly income and expenses for Amina, Mali and Beatrice.

	Amina	**Mali**	**Beatrice**

Income	\$2150	\$1800	\$2075
Needs and savings	\$507.98	\$230.67	\$409.99
Disposable income			

a How much disposable income do they each have each month?
Show your working and write the values in the bottom row of the table.

b Who has the highest disposable income?

____

c Who has the lowest disposable income?

____

Having higher earnings does not necessarily mean having a higher disposable income.

If a family that earns a lot of money spends more of their money on fixed expenses than a family that earns less money, then the higher earning family might actually have a lower disposable income each month.

2 Kai's family earns $4500 per month. Their fixed expenses each month are:

$1900 on rent
$900 on bills
$500 on transportation
$200 on insurance

Heinz's family earns $3200 per month. Their fixed expenses each month are:

$1100 on rent
$600 on bills
$200 on transportation
$100 on insurance

a Which family is the higher earning family?

____

b Which family has the highest disposable income each month?

There are two ways to increase disposable income. You can either earn more money, or you can spend less money on bills and fixed expenses.

3 How could Kai's family reduce their fixed expenses to increase their disposable income?

Discuss with a partner.

4 Heinz's family would like to increase their income so that their fixed expenses only account for 50% of their monthly earnings. How much would they need to earn to achieve this?

Saving and investing goals

1 Bolu earns \$400 per month. She wants to save up to buy a new bicycle. Her target is to save \$520.

a How many months will it take Bolu to reach her savings target of \$520 if each month she saves:

i 10% of her monthly income

ii 20% of her monthly income?

b What will Bolu need to consider when deciding how much to save each month?

Discuss with a partner.

The 50/30/20 principle states that you should save 20% of your income. However, this principle is just a guideline. Saving more money decreases the percentage of your income that you spend on either needs or wants by a corresponding amount.

2 At the start of the year, Lena saves 20% of her monthly salary of €500. She then increases the amount she saves by 1% each month for a year.

a How much did Lena save in the first month of the year?

b How much did Lena save in month 11?

c How much did Lena save, in total, during the year?

An **emergency fund** is a sum of money that is set aside to be used in the case of an emergency or a loss of income.

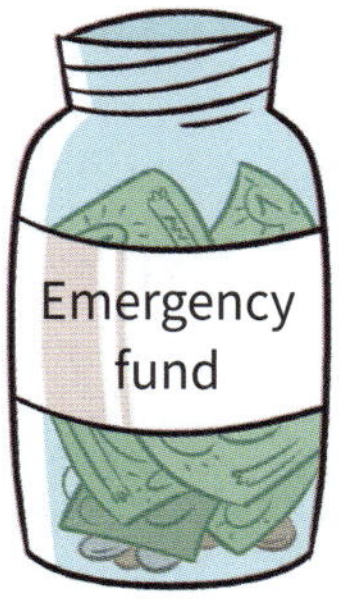

3 **a** Jing earns \$1450 per month. Her fixed expenses are \$900 per month. She wants to set aside an emergency fund **worth** 3 months of her fixed expenses.

What is the minimum number of full months Jing needs to save for in order to reach her target of a 3-month emergency fund, if she saves:

i 20% of her monthly salary

ii 30% of her monthly salary?

b Jing wants to increase her emergency fund to be worth 6 months of her fixed expenses. To do this, she plans to save 40% of her monthly salary.

Is this possible? Explain your answer.

A fun way to save money is to do a savings challenge, rather than save a fixed amount of money every month. This type of challenge can help to motivate you to save. It also enables you to start saving small amounts and then to increase the amount you save.

4 Starting in January, Omar decides to save \$10 in month one, \$20 in month two, \$30 in month three, and so on. He continues this saving pattern for one year, increasing the amount he saves by \$10 each month.

How much money will Omar save, in total, over one year?

Creating your own budget

1 Ravi has a monthly salary of $2500.

Use the 50/30/20 principle to calculate how much Ravi should spend on his needs and his wants and how much he should save each month.

Needs	Wants	Savings

2 Ravi is thinking about his expenses and his disposable income.

a Use the table to categorize Ravi's expenses into needs and wants. Write how much Ravi is currently spending, in total, on his needs and his wants.

	Needs	Wants
Total ($)		

b Is the money Ravi is currently spending on his expenses within his monthly budget, according to the 50/30/20 principle? Explain your answer.

c How would you recommend that Ravi could reduce his monthly **expenditure**?

Discuss with a partner.

3 **a** What would you like to save up money for?

How much do you think this might cost?

Discuss with a partner

b Create a savings challenge to enable you to save a target amount over one month by setting aside a realistic amount of money each day. Use the single month calendar template to fill in the amounts. Then work out the total amount you could save.

1	2	3	4	5	6	7
8	9	10	11	12	13	14
15	16	17	18	19	20	21
22	23	24	25	26	27	28
29	30	31				

Total: $

c How many months would it take you to save up for the item you thought of in part **a**?

3 The money system

What is the economy?

The **economy** is a big system that involves jobs, businesses, and spending money. Everything from the food we eat to the clothes we wear is part of the economy.

1 Fill in the blanks to describe how an economy can change. Choose words from the box below.

If businesses make ______________ money, they are able to pay their workers ______________ money, and their workers will have ______________ money to spend. This will cause the economy to ______________.

If businesses make ______________ money, they will need to pay their workers ______________ money, and their workers will have ______________ money to spend. This will cause the economy to ______________.

more **less** **grow** **more** **shrink** **less** **more** **less**

An economy is formed from different groups.

Producers make **goods** and provide services, such as food, toys and banking.

Consumers buy and use these goods and services.

In the United Kingdom, the **government** makes rules and decisions to keep the economy working well. The government might, for example, raise or lower **taxes**, increase or decrease public spending, or raise or lower the supply of money into the system.

2 The United Kingdom has a tax called Value Added Tax (VAT). This tax is included in the price of many goods and services. In 2023, VAT in the UK was 20%.

The cost of a pair of jeans in 2023 without VAT was £80.

a Work out the amount of VAT for this pair of jeans.

b What is the total cost of the pair of jeans including VAT?

c Is there a VAT in the country where you live? If yes, what is the current VAT rate?

____

Demand describes how much people want to buy something.

Supply describes how much of that thing is available.

When demand is high and supply is low, prices usually increase.

When supply is high and demand is low, prices might decrease.

3 *Discuss the following questions with a partner.*

- **a** *What types of things do you think might be in high demand?*
- **b** *What types of things do you think might be in low demand?*
- **c** *What could affect the supply of a product?*
- **d** *What could affect the demand for a product?*

4 100 tickets are available to buy for a concert. The original price of a ticket is $300. The first half of the tickets sell for full price. Due to increased demand, the event organizers then decide to sell the second half of the tickets for 15% more.

a What is the new price of a ticket?

b How much do all the tickets sell for, in total?

c How much more money does the event organizer make compared to if all the tickets were sold at the original price?

Trade is when people exchange goods and services with each other.

Money makes it easier for people to trade, because money has value.

5 Jasmine owns a company that sells eggs. One week, she has 30 500 eggs. She would like to make $8000 from the sale of these eggs.

a How much should Jasmine price each egg to make her target amount? Give your answer in dollars to the nearest cent.

$

b Jasmine usually sells the eggs in boxes of 12 eggs. She sells each box for $3. How much more or less than her target of $8000 does she make by selling the eggs in boxes rather than individually?

$

What is money?

Money is a **unit of account**. This allows us to know how much things are worth in comparison with other things.

1 It takes Gareth two years to decorate his house. In the first year, he starts painting. He has $250 to spend on paint. Each can of paint costs $9.00.

a How many cans of paint can Gareth buy?

b Gareth buys as many cans of paint as he can with $250. How much of his paint budget does he have left over?

$

c Gareth's house cost $250 000. How many more times expensive was his house than the total cost of paint?

d A painter and decorator **quotes** Gareth $25 000 to paint his house.

i What proportion of his house cost is this?

ii Do you think this represents good value? Discuss with a partner.

Inflation refers to the rise in prices over time.

2 In the second year of decorating his house, Gareth returns to the paint store to buy some more cans of paint. Due to inflation, the price of paint has increased by 2%.

a What is the new cost of each can of paint?

b Gareth needs to buy 10 cans of paint. How much more will these cans of paint cost than if he had bought them in the first year?

3 The price of a can of paint is $9.00. Below are the annual inflation rates of five different countries:

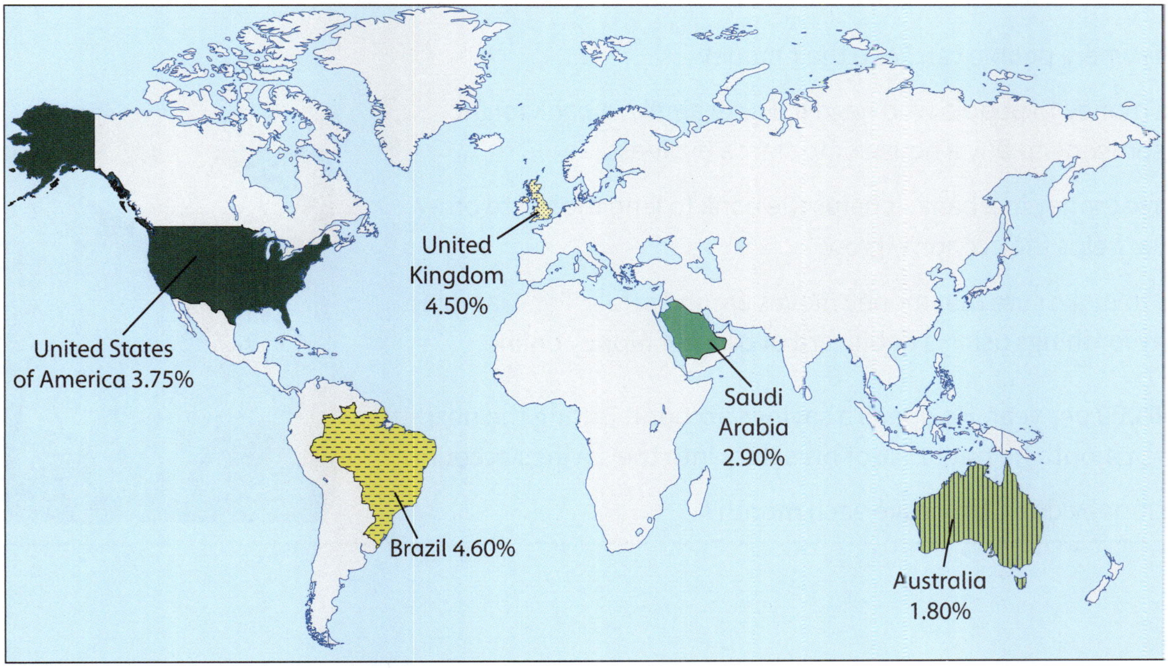

Given the inflation rates shown, how much will a can of paint cost in each country after one year?

Throughout history, different forms of money have been used.

Coins are some of the oldest forms of money. Coins were first developed in about 600 BC.

Paper money was first introduced in the 1200s, partially because coins were difficult to use and heavy to carry.

Money transfers through the use of debit cards were introduced in the 1960s.

Cryptocurrencies were introduced in the 2000s.

4 a To the nearest 100 years, how many years older are coins than cryptocurrencies?

b To the nearest 100 years, for how many years was paper money used before debit cards were introduced?

What are banks?

Banks are places where people can keep their money.

Banks also lend money to people who need it. For example, a bank might lend money to someone to buy a house or to start a business.

When people save money in a bank, it helps the bank to lend money to other people and it also helps the economy grow.

Banks also help to make sure that money moves around safely. For example, when people pay for things using a debit card or transfer money online.

1 Amir earns $50 000 per year. He opens a savings account. During the next 18 months, each month he puts 15% of his salary into the savings account.

a How much money does Amir save each month?

b How much money does Amir save, in total, during the 18 months?

c Amir is saving up to buy a new car that costs $15 000. How many months will it take him to save up to buy the car?

d Amir decides that he would like to buy a new car within 12 months because he needs to travel for work. What are his options? Discuss with a partner.

Business banking is a special type of bank account for companies instead of individual people. Business banking helps businesses manage their money. For example, when a business receives payments from customers or when they pay bills. Businesses can also use services such as business loans to help their business grow.

2 Camille owns a bakery. She takes out a business loan of $5000 to buy new baking equipment.

a If Camille repays $200 each month, how many months will it take her to repay the full loan amount?

[ ] months

b Camille draws a line graph to track how much money she has to pay back. Complete the line graph.

c Camille realizes that she can afford to pay back $300 each month. Draw a line on the graph to show this.

d How much faster could Camille repay the full loan amount by paying $300 per month instead of $200 per month? Give your answer to the nearest number of months.

☐ months

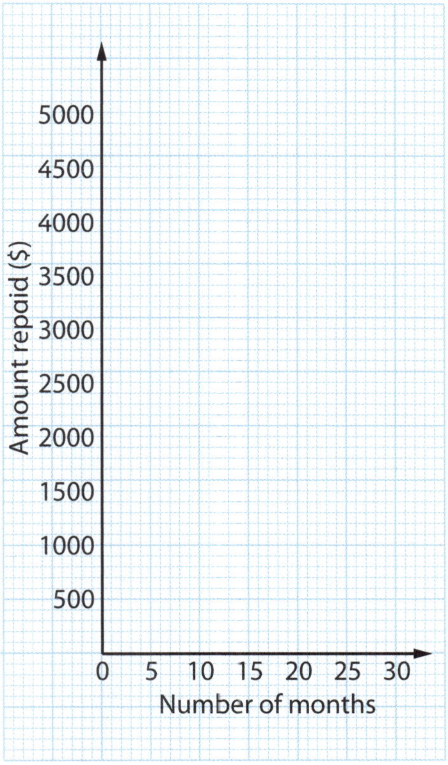

Investment banks act as **financial advisors** for governments and businesses, helping them to make important money decisions. Investment banks can help with **mergers** (when companies combine) and **acquisitions** (when one company buys another company).

3 Discuss the following questions with a partner.

Can you think of any real life examples of when two big companies have merged?
What other big financial decisions might a company need to make?
What big financial decisions might a government need to make?

4 Here are four different companies and their **net worth**:

Company A ($54 billion)
Company B ($43 billion)
Company C ($38 billion)
Company D ($58 billion)

Each company is considering a merger with one of the other companies.

In the table below, list all of the different merger options in order of total net worth.

Companies merging	Net worth

What is a currency?

Different countries around the world use different **currencies**. For example, the United States uses dollars, Malaysia uses ringgit, and Ghana uses cedi.

1 Draw lines to match each currency to the correct country.

 Argentina	euro
 Sweden	dirham
 Nigeria	dollar
 Brazil	krona
 China	renminbi
 Japan	rupee
 Canada	naira
 Germany	yen
 Pakistan	real
 United Arab Emirates	peso

Exchange rates show how much one currency is worth compared to other currencies. For example, if the exchange rate between euros and US dollars is 1.07, it means that €1 is worth $1.07.

Exchange rates change over time based on factors such as supply and demand, economic conditions and government policies.

Understanding currency and exchange rates helps people know how much things cost when they travel or do business internationally.

	Amount
US dollars	1
Malaysian ringgits	4.76
Saudi Arabian riyals	3.75
Kuwaiti dinars	0.31
Kenyan shillings	134.97

2 The exchange rates between some currencies are shown in the table on the right.

Use these exchange rates to calculate, to two decimal places:

a how many Saudi Arabian riyals you would get for 100 US dollars

b how many Kenyan shillings you would get for 50 US dollars

c how many Kuwaiti dinars you would get for 200 US dollars

d how many US dollars you would get for 100 Malaysian ringgits.

3 Sabina is going on holiday to France.

a Before she goes on holiday, Sabina needs to exchange $100 into euros at the **bureau de change**. The exchange rate is $1 = €0.93. How many euros will Sabina receive?

b At the end of her holiday, Sabina has €25 left. The bureau de change will buy back euros. The exchange rate they offer is €1 = $1.02. How many dollars will Sabina receive?

Give your answer to the nearest cent.

4 a Sabina is looking online for accommodation for her holiday. She will be in France for four nights. She has an accommodation budget of $320 for her stay. Sabina finds a hotel online that costs €80 per night. Is her budget enough for her to stay in this hotel?

b With her $320 budget, what is the maximum amount per night that Sabina can pay for a hotel?

Give your answer in euros to the nearest cent.

What is insurance?

Insurance is protection against events that could cause a financial loss. To get insurance, you pay a certain amount of money, called a **premium**, to a company. The insurance company then provides cover against specific events happening.

Car insurance is a legal requirement for anyone who drives a car. You pay a premium to the insurance company. The insurance company then provides cover against specific events. The premium you pay depends on different things. The insurance company will help cover the costs, but you usually still have to pay some money, called the **excess**.

1 **a** What factors do you think affect a person's car insurance premium? Discuss with a partner.

b Omar bought a car **insurance policy** for $400 for one year. The insurance company estimates that there is a 2% chance of Omar having an accident during this year. What is the chance that Omar will *not* have a car accident this year? Express your answer as a fraction in its simplest form.

c Jenny wants to buy car insurance for her new car.

Insurance company A offers her a policy for $500 per year, with no excess.

Insurance company B offers her a policy for $450 per year, plus a $200 excess in case of an accident. Insurance data states there is a 25% chance that a driver with Jenny's profile will have an accident in the next year. Which insurance company would you recommend for Jenny? Explain your answer.

d Jenny's friend Sara is also looking for car insurance. She receives the following quotes.

Which of the deals would you recommend that Sara purchases? Discuss with a partner.

It is advisable to buy travel insurance when you travel. You pay a premium to the insurance company. Your travel insurance policy will usually cover specific events. You need to be careful when you choose a policy that it is suitable for your travel plans.

2 **a** What different events do you think travel insurance policies might cover? Discuss with a partner.

b Harriet is going on a trip to London. She decides to buy travel insurance for $50. While travelling, her suitcase is lost. The replacement suitcase and items cost $300, but, because she has travel insurance, the insurance company covers 80% of the cost. How much money does Harriet need to pay for the replacement suitcase and items?

c **i** Circle the correct words to make the following sentence true.

Frequent claims might result in higher lower premiums due to increased decreased risk.

ii Discuss with a partner why this sentence is true.

Home insurance protects your house and the items inside your house in case of unexpected events. When you buy home insurance, you pay a premium to an insurance company. In return, if your home or the items inside your home are damaged, the insurance company helps to cover the costs to repair or replace the items up to a certain limit.

3 **a** Discuss the following questions with a partner.

What different events do you think home insurance policies cover?
What factors do you think would increase the cost of someone's home insurance?

b Mohammed has home insurance worth $300 000. A flood causes $50 000 worth of damage to his property. His insurance policy covers flooding, but he has to pay an excess fee of $2000.

i What percentage of the overall damage is this excess fee?

ii What effect do you think this will have on Mohammed's home insurance premium the following year? Discuss with a partner.

What is the stock market?

The **stock market** is a big marketplace where people buy and sell ownership in companies. When you buy a stock, you essentially buy a small part of that company. The value of the stock can go up or down based on how well the company is doing and what people think the company will do in the future based on current information. **Investors** try to make money by buying stocks when the price is low and selling these stocks when the price is high.

1 **a** *Classic Cars to Go* is a large national company that specializes in selling classic cars. Use the table to sort the following scenarios into things that might make the price of the company's stocks increase or decrease. Write each letter (A–H) in the correct column.

Think about news events, industry trends and the company's financial reports.

- **A** The company recalls 500 cars to repair a problem with the engines.
- **B** The company's recent car sales are much higher than expected.
- **C** A new competitor starts selling classic cars for a cheaper price.
- **D** A storm damages the company's warehouse.
- **E** The company gets a very good review on the leading classic cars website.
- **F** The company's biggest customer, a classic car reseller, stops buying cars.
- **G** The company is bought by a leading international car dealership.
- **H** There is a national news report on the increased popularity of classic car ownership.

Increase stock price	Decrease stock price

b Lili invested \$5000 in *Classic Cars to Go*. In year 1, her investment grew by 10%. She decided to reinvest her profits with her initial investment for another year. In year 2, her investments grew by 15%. Lili continues to invest for another year. Unfortunately her investments decrease in value by 5%. How much does she have, in total, at the end of year 3?

An **investment broker** helps individuals or organizations invest their money. They provide advice and assistance to their **client** on buying and selling financial **assets**. Brokers also monitor market trends and help clients to make informed decisions to grow their wealth.

2 **a** Chaiya decides to invest $12 000 in the stock market through an online broker. The broker charges a commission fee of 5% on all transactions. Chaiya invests $1000 a month for a year, paying the 5% fee each time. How much does he pay in fees, in total, in one year?

$ ______

b Chaiya changes to use a commission free broker. This costs an annual fee as a percentage of the investment. If he invests $12 000 and pays 10% of his investment in fees, how much does he pay in fees per year?

$ ______

c Chiaya is interested in **socially responsible investments**. He asks his broker to prioritize companies that show an awareness of social and **environmental** issues. What type of companies, or features of companies, might the broker look for? Discuss with a partner.

Buying the shares of multiple companies at the same time is called a stock portfolio. Investors create portfolios of stocks so that they can spread their money across multiple companies. This is called **diversification**. It can make holding individual stocks less risky.

3 **a** Why do you think spreading investment over multiple different companies makes investing less risky? Discuss with a partner.

b Marcus has a $30 000 portfolio of stocks of the companies listed below. The percentages of his money that he has in each company are shown. Complete the table to show how much money he has in each stock.

Company	Percentage of total stock portfolio	Value ($)
A	15%	
B	10%	
C	25%	
D	5%	
E	20%	
F	7%	
G	13%	
H	5%	

c Draw a pie chart to help Martin visualize his portfolio.

4 Earning money

Earning pocket money

1 Mauro and Laura are brother and sister. They both earn pocket money by doing jobs at home. Here is an earnings chart that they created with their parents.

Job	Earnings
Dusting	\$2.50
Cleaning the bathroom	\$3.25
Mowing the lawn	\$7.50
Taking out the rubbish	\$1.20
Making the bed	\$2.25
Washing up	\$1.75
Hanging up the laundry	\$2
Vacuuming	\$2.50

a Why do you think Mauro and Laura's parents ask their children to do jobs to earn their pocket money, rather than just giving them pocket money each week?

b One week, Mauro does the washing up three times. He also does the vacuuming and dusting once. Laura mows the lawn, takes out the rubbish twice and cleans the bathroom. How much do they each earn in pocket money that week?

Mauro

Laura

2 Laura would like to save up her pocket money to buy a pair of sneakers. The sneakers cost $50.

a Laura normally earns $10 pocket money a week. She saves 20% of this money. How many weeks will it take her to reach her savings goal?

[ ] weeks

b Look back at the earnings chart. What combination of jobs could Laura do to earn $10 in a week?

Work with a partner to list as many possible combinations as you can.

____

____

____

c Laura's parents book a holiday for the summer. Laura would like to buy the sneakers before they go on holiday in 16 weeks. What different options does Laura have to achieve this new savings goal?

Discuss with a partner.

3 Mauro would like to earn $500 pocket money in one year.

How many weeks are there in one year?

a How much pocket money would he need to earn every week to achieve this goal? Give your answer to the nearest cent.

b During the year, there are four weeks when Mauro does no jobs. How much more pocket money will he need to earn every week that he does do jobs to achieve his goal?

c What if there were eight weeks when Mauro does no job? How much more pocket money would he need to earn every week? Give your answer to the nearest cent.

Earning money in a job

An annual salary is the amount of money a person earns from their job in one year. It is a fixed payment, agreed upon by the **employer** and the **employee**, for the work done during one year, regardless of how many hours they work each week or month.

1 Lina, a software engineer from Germany, earns an annual salary of €60 000. How much does she earn:

a per month € ______

b per week? € ______

In most countries, part of the money a person earns goes to the government as **income tax**.

In the UK, the money paid in income tax helps the government pay for things such as schools, hospitals and roads. The amount of income tax you pay depends on how much you earn. Generally, higher earners pay a higher **tax rate**. In 2025/2026, the tax bands in the UK were:

Band	Taxable income	Tax rate
Personal allowance	Up to £12 570	0%
Basic rate	£12 571 to £37 700	20%
Higher rate	£37 701 to £125 140	40%
Additional rate	Over £125 140	45%

2 Use the information about UK tax bands to complete the table below.

Person	Amount of income tax paid	Pay, after tax deducted
Rufus, a teacher, earns £36 000		
Gladys, a nurse, earns £27 000		
Karl, a creative director, earns £130 000		
Laila, a lawyer, earns £65 000		

Everyone has the same personal allowance and the higher rates of tax are only paid on earnings over the basic tax rate.

Some people are paid an hourly rate for the work they do. For example, if a person with an hourly rate of $10 works for 5 hours, they will earn $50, in total.

3 **a** Alexander is looking for a freelance graphic designer to design a company logo. He receives two estimates from two different freelancers.

Belinda charges $28 per hour. She estimates that the logo will take a total of 12 hours to design.

Marcus charges $30 per hour for design work and 50% of his hourly rate for any additional amends. He estimates that he would spend 10 hours designing the logo, and another 2 hours on amends.

Which freelance graphic designer, Belinda or Marcus, would charge the lowest amount to do the work?

____

b Is cost the only thing Alexander should consider when deciding which freelancer to choose? Discuss with a partner.

It is common for companies to offer their employees retirement savings plans. This is money that people save during their working years to pay for their living costs after they stop working.

4 Yohan, a data analyst, starts saving for his retirement at the age of 25. He plans to retire when he is 65 years old.

a How much money would Yohan have in his retirement savings account when he is 65 if he saves $500 every month?

$ [ ]

b Yohan would like to have $300 000 in his retirement savings when he retires. How much extra would he need to save each month?

[ ]

c Instead of increasing his monthly retirement savings, Yohan could save more money by working for more years. If he saves $500 a month, until what age would he need to work to have $300 000 of retirement savings?

[ ]

Earning money from a business

An **entrepreneur** makes money from a business. They provide a product or service that people pay for. The money they receive from selling goods and services is called **revenue**. The entrepreneur aims to earn more money than the cost of making or providing that product or service.

1 Jack owns a small café. Each day, on average, he earns $500 selling sandwiches and drinks. However, he also needs to pay his staff $200 per day.

a What percentage of his revenue does Jack spend on staff wages?

Jack speaks to a friend who advises him to keep his staffing costs to 30% of his revenue or less.

b Following this advice, what is the maximum Jack should pay his staff, in total, on an average day?

c Jack pays his staff $12 per hour. What is the maximum number of hours that Jack should pay his staff to work between them, in order to achieve his new staffing cost target?

d What could be a disadvantage of reducing the staff working hours?

Discuss with a partner.

Being self-employed is slightly different to being an entrepreneur. Typically, a self-employed person works on their own to deliver a product, service or trade. A self-employed person is in control of their own work and schedule. They can choose what type of work they want to do and how much they want to charge for their work. They are also responsible for managing their business finances and finding their own customers.

2 **a** Javier, a self-employed electrician, charges $60 per hour for his services. He also charges a $100 callout fee whenever he is booked to do a job. Last week, he worked on various electrical jobs for a total of 15 hours and received 4 bookings.

How much money did Javier earn, in total, that week?

b Eva is a **self-employed** freelance editor. She is paid on a project basis. She charges:

$300 for an article $150 for a short blog post $800 for an ebook

Last month, she edited three articles, one ebook and two short blog posts.

How much money did Eva earn last month?

$ ______

Think about earnings, time management, holidays, and so on.

c Discuss with a partner the advantages and disadvantages of working in full-time employment versus working on a self-employed basis.

Business profit is the money an individual or company earns after subtracting all of the **business expenses** from the revenue.

3 Jack works out the proportion of his revenue that he spends on each of his business expenses in the café's first year.

Ingredients 11%
Staff 40%
Rent 20%
WiFi 1%
Insurance 2%
Utilities 4%

Remember that Jack's revenue is $500 per day.

a Jack's café is open for 20 days per month. Use the information above to complete Jack's annual profit statement for year 1. One row has been done for you.

b What proportion of his overall revenue does Jack's **profit** represent? Give your answer as a percentage.

______ %

c In year 2, Jack's revenue decreases by 15% due to a new competitor in the local area. His expenses also increase by 12%. How much profit/loss does Jack make in year 2?

$ ______

d Discuss with a partner the different ways that Jack could increase his **profitability**.

Annual profit statement	
	Year 1
Sales revenue	
Costs	
Ingredients	
Staff costs	
Rent	$24 000
WiFi	
Insurance	
Utilities	
Profit	

Earning money from property

Earning money from renting out a property means that the owner of the property does not live in the property. Instead, someone else pays the owner a fixed amount of money each month to live there. The money paid to live in the property is called **rent**. The owner of the property can use this rent money to pay for expenses such as repairs, property taxes, and other expenses. Any money left over is their profit.

1 Sandra owns an apartment that she rents out to **tenants**. She charges $1200 per month in rent. After deducting $150 per month for property taxes, $100 for maintenance, and $500 for the mortgage payment, how much profit does Sandra make from renting out the apartment for one year?

You can earn money from owning a property that increases in value. This means making a profit by selling the property for a higher price than you originally paid for the property. For example, if you buy a house for $200 000 and sell it a few years later for $250 000, you have earned $50 000.

2 Sandra bought the apartment five years ago for $300 000. In those five years, the value of her apartment has increased by 20%. She decides to sell the apartment.

a With the 20% increase in value, how much does she sell the apartment for?

b Including the profit from renting the property you calculated in question 1, and the profit from selling the apartment, what is Sandra's overall average yearly profit from this property over these five years?

It is also possible to earn money from **renovating** a property. This involves buying a property that needs repairs or improvements, making the necessary improvements, and then selling the property for a higher price than the total cost of the purchase and the renovation.

3 Using the profit from the apartment, Sandra decides to buy a house to renovate. She buys a house for $120 000 but it needs a lot of work. She spends $45 000 on renovating the house. After six months, she sells the renovated house for $250 000.

What is Sandra's profit from renovating and selling the property?

Property development is another way of earning money from property. It means buying land, building or improving structures on it, and then selling or renting out those properties for a profit. It involves tasks such as designing buildings, getting permits, hiring construction workers, and overseeing the project. The profit comes from selling the developed properties for more than the cost of buying the land and completing the construction.

4 After successfully renovating the house, Sandra decides to start a property development business. She buys some land for $175 000 and spends $500 000 to build four houses on the land. She then sells each house for $225 000.

a How much profit does she make per house?

b The development project takes one and a half years to complete.

What is Sandra's average profit per year for this project?

Freelance work

A freelance taxi driver earns money by charging people for rides. Each time the taxi driver gives someone a ride, the customer pays the driver a **fare**. The more rides the taxi driver gives, the more money they can earn. However, they also have to consider expenses such as fuel and maintenance for their taxi. They need to subtract their expenses from their earnings to calculate their overall profit.

1 a Emma works as a freelance taxi driver in New York. On Monday, she gives 10 rides. She receives the following fares:

$27.95, $16.75, $39.28, $18.34, $10.12, $32.65, $25.87, $19.89, $41.76, $33.85

However, on that day she spends $54.25 on fuel and $15 on taxi maintenance. What is her overall profit for that day?

$ ____

b Here is a table showing Emma's fares and expenses for the week. Fill in the values for Monday from part **a**. Then fill in the missing values for the other days.

	Monday	Tuesday	Wednesday	Thursday	Friday	Saturday	Sunday
Fares ($)		323.15	167.89		123.05		198.65
Fuel ($)			40.73	66.75	34.30	106.22	43.40
Maintenance ($)		50	140	0		10	0
Profit ($)		198.90		231.71	-41.25	258.40	

c What was Emma's total profit (or loss) for the week?

$ ____

Content creators earn money by creating content, such as videos, articles, or other online content, that people enjoy and find valuable. When people watch, read, or interact with the content, the creator can earn money through advertisements, sponsorships, or selling products. The more popular the content becomes, the more money the creator can earn.

2 a Arjun is a content creator. What guidelines should Arjun be aware of when creating and sharing videos online? Discuss with a partner.

b Arjun earns $1.50 for every 100 views on his online video sharing platform. His latest video received 1.2 million views. How much money did he earn from that video, in total?

$ ____

c 20% of the 1.2 million viewers left Arjun a comment on his video. Write the ratio of viewers who left a comment to viewers who did not leave a comment in its simplest form.

A freelance web developer creates websites and applications for people or businesses. The web developer earns money by creating websites that work well and look good. The more websites they create, the more money they can earn.

3 **a** Nathalie is a freelance web developer based in Paris. She charges €500 to build a basic website for a local bakery. The bakery owner then refers Nathalie to three other businesses in the local area. Nathalie charges an additional 5% for each subsequent website she builds for these three businesses. How much money does Nathalie earn, in total, from building websites for the bakery and the three referred businesses?

b Nathalie's friend suggests that Nathalie charges an hourly rate instead of a fixed fee for her services. What do you think the advantages and disadvantages of this might be?

Discuss with a partner.

Nathalie does some research online to see what other local web developers charge. Here are some adverts that she finds:

c How much do you think Nathalie should charge per hour, based on the competition?

Explain your reasoning.

d Assume that Nathalie charges the hourly rate you suggested in part **c**. If each website build from part **a** takes her 12 hours, how much more would Nathalie earn by charging an hourly rate rather than a fixed fee?

euros

Future career choices

1 a *There are many different **career paths** and ways of earning money. Discuss the following questions with a partner.*

How do you think the world of work is changing?

What skills are you likely to need to be well prepared for these changes?

b Make a list of your key strengths and favourite subjects.

What **career** options might these lead on to?

c Salaries are one aspect to consider when looking at your career options. What other factors should you take into account?

2 Stefan is researching different career paths. He finds the following information online:

Job role	Dentist	Plumber	Engineer	Customer services advisor
Training required (unpaid)	5 years	2 years	3 years	0 years (on the job training)
Average weekly hours	50	40	35	35
Average salary	\$69 000	\$33 000	\$48 000	\$19 700

a For each job, taking into consideration the time spent training, what would Stefan's average annual salary be over:

i 6 years

ii 8 years

iii 10 years

iv Discuss, with a partner, how the mean salaries change over time.

b Which of the above careers would you most like to do, and why?

Discuss with a partner.

3 Choose one of the careers from question **2**. Design a poster to show the benefits of your chosen career. Think about the given information, as well as what you know about the career.

5 Spending money wisely

Discounts

A discount is a reduction in the original price of an item. A discount is often shown as a percentage. The discount indicates how much less the item now costs. Discounts can be applied to individual items or to the total purchase.

An item costs $10. If a 20% discount is applied, then the item will now cost $8.

1 Fatima is shopping at a supermarket.

a She finds a box of chocolates that originally cost $5. There is a 15% discount. How much will Fatima pay for the box of chocolates after the discount is applied?

$ ☐

b She decides to buy two bags of apples. The bags of apples originally cost $2 each. There is a 10% discount on her total purchase. How much will Fatima save?

$ ☐

c Discounts can also be given as fractions. Write the following discounts in order, smallest first.

$\frac{2}{3}$ **25%** $\frac{1}{3}$ **20%** $\frac{1}{2}$ **30%**

........, ..., ..., ..., ..., ...,

Coupons are vouchers or codes that give customers discounts or special offers on purchases. Sometimes, stores send coupons directly to customers. When using a coupon, the discount is applied to the total cost of the items being purchased.

2 Fatima receives some coupons to save money on her shopping.

a She wants to buy a pair of shoes priced at $30. She has this coupon:
How much will Fatima save by using the coupon?

$ ☐

SHOE STORE
20%
off shoes

b She then finds three books, each priced at $10. She has this coupon:
How much will Fatima pay for the three books using this coupon?

$ ☐

BEST BOOKS
$5
off total purchase

Stores sometimes sell damaged but functional items at **reduced** prices to clear space in their store room. The reduced prices make these items more affordable for customers who are willing to accept the minor damage.

3 Fatima is shopping for electronic goods. She is interested in some discounted items.

a She finds a camera with a broken strap. The camera originally cost \$150. With a 15% discount, how much will Fatima save compared to buying the camera at full price?

\$

b She also sees a laptop with a scratch on the screen. The laptop originally cost \$500. There is a 25% discount for the damaged laptop. Fatima also has a \$50 off coupon. How much will she pay if the coupon is applied to the discounted price of the laptop?

\$

c For each scenario, discuss with a partner whether you would buy the imperfect item or the perfect item.

- A phone with a damaged case for \$500 or a perfect phone and case for \$1000
- A pair of sneakers with a mark on the toe for \$100 or a perfect pair of sneakers for \$150
- A book with some torn pages for \$5 or a perfect book for \$16

Online voucher codes are special codes that customers can use during online shopping to access discounts or other promotional offers. These codes are usually provided by retailers or through promotional campaigns.

4 Fatima has some voucher codes to use when shopping online.

a She finds a pair of shoes that cost \$40 and a bag that costs \$30. She has a voucher code for a \$10 discount on orders over \$50. How much will Fatima pay for both items after applying the code?

\$

b Fatima sees a laptop priced at \$550, with a voucher code offering a 15% discount. How much will she save on the price of the laptop?

\$

c Fatima is considering subscribing to a meal kit retailer. The meal kits cost \$28.00 a month. The minimum subscription is for one year. There is a 30% discount code for new customers for their first 3 months. The remaining months are then full price. If Fatima subscribes using the discount, how much will she pay, in total, for one year?

Promotions

Buy One, Get One (also known as BOGO) promotions give customers the opportunity to purchase one item and receive another item of equal or lesser value for free or at a discounted price. These promotions are commonly seen in supermarkets and retail stores.

1 Michel would like to use some BOGO promotions during his shopping trip.

a Michel finds a BOGO promotion on apples. The offer is:

GOOD BUYS — Buy one bag of apples for $3 and get a second bag of apples for free

Using this offer, how much does Michel pay for two bags of apples?

$

b Michel also finds a BOGO promotion on shampoo bottles. The individual shampoo bottles are priced at $5 each. The offer is:

GOOD BUYS — Buy one bottle of shampoo and get the second bottle for half price

Using this offer, how much does Michel pay for two bottles of shampoo?

$

c Michel then finds a BOGO promotion on T-shirts. The offer is:

GOOD BUYS — Buy one T-shirt for $10 and get 25% off a second T-shirt of the same price

Michel buys two T-shirts. Using this offer, how much does he pay, in total?

$

Three for two promotions offer customers the opportunity to buy three items and only pay the price of two of the items. If the items have different prices, the customer usually pays for the two most expensive items, and the least expensive item is free.

2 Michel sees some three for two promotions at a stationery store.

a Michel buys three packs of pencils, each priced at $2. There is a three for two promotion on the packs of pencils. Using this promotion, how much does he pay, in total?

$

b Michel sees three books, priced at $5, $7, and $8 respectively. There is a three for two promotion on the books. Using this promotion, how much does he save?

$ ______

c Michel finds three sets of paints, priced at $13, $17 and $20 respectively. There is a three for two promotion on the sets of paint. Alternatively, Michel has a 25% off coupon for total spend on paint. The three for two promotion and coupon cannot be used together. Should Michel use the three for two promotion or the coupon? Explain your answer.

______

______

During holiday seasons, stores often use special promotions, such as discounts and BOGO offers, to attract customers and increase sales.

3 Michel has a budget of $50 to buy holiday items. He sees the following discounts on his favourite online store:

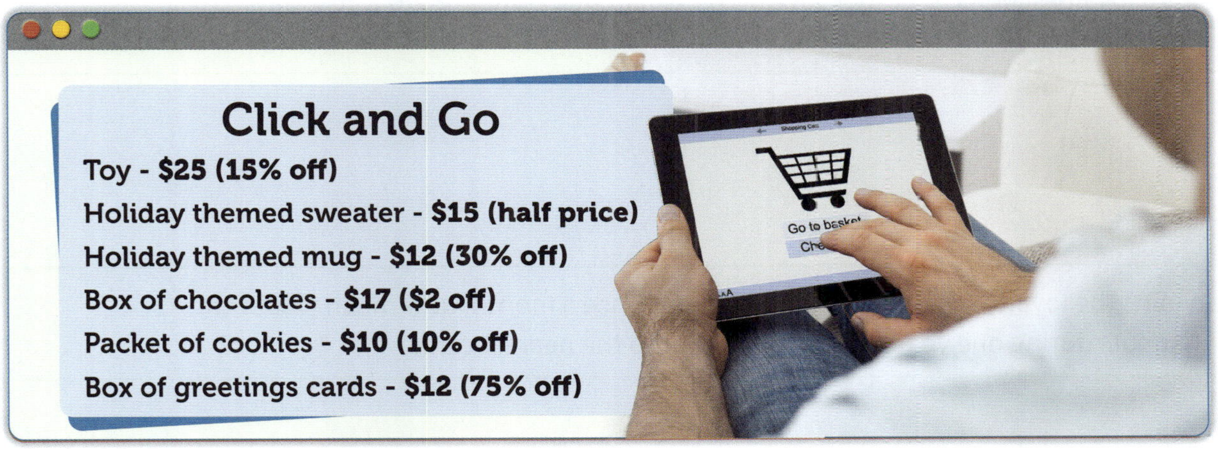

For the offers to apply, a maximum of one of each item can be bought.

What combination of items can Michel buy within his budget? List as many possibilities as you can.

Loyalty and reward schemes

Loyalty schemes reward customers for continuing to shop at the store. Customers usually sign up for these schemes and receive a membership card or account. The benefits of joining a loyalty scheme include discounts, free products or enhanced services.

1 Before joining the loyalty scheme at her favourite salon, Sharon wants to assess the benefits.

a Sharon discovers that she will get a stamp on her loyalty card each time she has her hair cut. Once she receives eight stamps, her ninth haircut is free. If a haircut costs $72.50, how much would Sharon have to spend to receive a free haircut?

b Loyalty scheme members at the salon also receive a 15% discount off all haircuts. How much does a loyalty scheme member save on nine haircuts, compared to a customer who is not a member of the loyalty scheme?

c If Sharon joins the loyalty scheme and gets a haircut once a month, how much would she save on haircuts during one year? Give your answer to the nearest cent.

Rewards points are used to encourage customer loyalty. When a customer makes a purchase, they earn points based on the amount of money spent. The customer can collect these points over time. They can then exchange their points for various rewards, such as discounts, free products, or exclusive offers.

2 Sharon is a member of her local supermarket rewards scheme.

a As a rewards scheme member, she earns 1 point for every $5 she spends at the supermarket. During one visit to the supermarket she earns 40 points. How much money did Sharon spend to earn these points?

$

b She exchanges some of her points for a $20 discount voucher. Each point is worth $0.40 when exchanged. How many points does Sharon use to receive the $20 discount?

$ [ ]

c Sharon wants to exchange the rest of her points for a free grocery item worth $50. She has 100 points. How many more points does Sharon need to receive the free item?

$ [ ]

As members of an air miles reward scheme, customers earn air miles or points for their purchases, for example, when they buy flights. They can then exchange these air miles for free or discounted flights or for other travel-related expenses. The more air miles a customer earns, the more rewards they can receive.

3 Sharon is planning a holiday to Australia. She would like to use her air miles.

a Sharon earns 1 air mile for every $3 she spends using her debit card. After using her debit card for everyday purchases, she has earned 800 air miles. How much money did Sharon spend to earn these air miles?

b Sharon continues to collect air miles and then exchanges 50 000 air miles for a flight ticket to Australia. If each air mile is worth $0.04 when exchanged, what is the cost of the flight ticket?

c Sharon also wants to use her air miles to pay for a hotel in Australia. A hotel stay costs 3000 air miles. Sharon has 2500 air miles so far. If she receives 1 air mile for every $3 she spends, how much more does Sharon have to spend to have 3000 air miles?

New or second hand?

Buying **second hand** means buying items that have been previously owned by someone else.

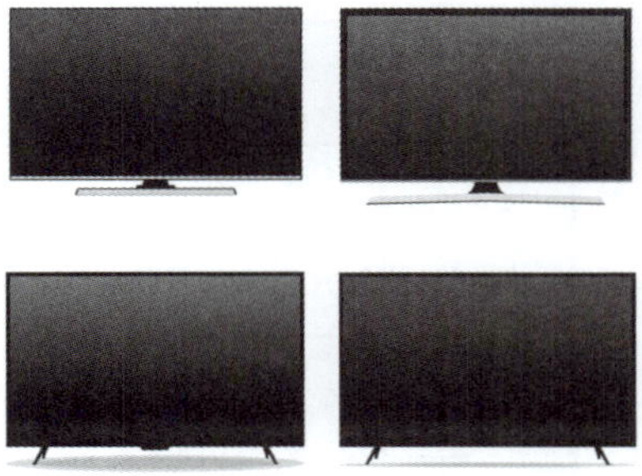

1 George is shopping for a second-hand television on a website.

a He finds one listed for $85.50. If the same model of television costs $279.25 new, how much money will he save by purchasing the television second hand?

b With the money he has saved, George decides to buy some games for his games console. If games cost $25 each, how many games can he buy with the money he saved?

At flea markets, sellers can sell their unwanted items. They can display their items for sale at prices they decide themselves.

2 a At a flea market, George buys seven books, priced at $4.25 each. He also buys eight books priced at $3.45 each. How much money does George spend on the books, in total?

b He then buys four T-shirts, priced at $6.75 each, and nine toys, priced at $3.35 each. How much money does George spend, in total, on the T-shirts and toys?

c George arrived at the flea market with $150 in his pocket. How much money does he have left after all of his purchases?

At a second hand electronics store, customers can trade their electronic devices in exchange for vouchers or cash. The store assesses the condition of the device to determine its value. The customer then receives an offer for the item. They can accept or decline the offer.

3 George goes to a second hand electronics store to trade in his smartphone.

a The store offers George an exchange of vouchers worth $338 to spend in the store. He would like to buy a new smartphone that costs $599.89 at the store. How much extra money would George need to pay as well as the vouchers?

b Alternatively, the store offers to buy George's smartphone for $280 cash. Online, the same new smartphone costs $510. Should George take the vouchers and buy the smartphone at the store, or take the cash and buy the smartphone online? Explain your answer.

Charity stores accept donations of second hand items from individuals in the community. They then sell these items to customers to make money for the charity.

4 George shops at charity stores because he can buy items for less money *and* support a good cause.

a He buys five items of clothing from a charity store. The prices of the items are shown:

$34.75 **$25.50** **$64.25** **$89.99** **$75.25**

The total cost of these items of clothing would be $820.35 if bought new. How much money does George save by buying these items at the charity store?

b Before shopping at charity stores, George spent, on average, $1500 on clothing every year. By buying some of his clothes at charity stores, George is able to spend 25% less on clothing per year. What is the average amount that George now spends on clothing each month?

Ways to spend less money

Price comparison websites collect and compare prices from various retailers. Users can search for a particular item and compare prices, features, and customer reviews across different sellers. Price comparison websites help users find the best deals.

1 Andreea uses a price comparison website to find the best deal on a new laptop. She finds three different models of laptop on the price comparison website:

	Laptop 1	Laptop 2	Laptop 3

Storage	256GB	512GB	1TB
Price	$500	$900	$1700

1TB = 1000GB

a Write the laptops in order of amount of storage per dollar, smallest first.

b Andreea decides to buy Laptop 2. However, six months ago, this laptop was reduced by 45% in a seasonal sale. What was its price at the time?

c The current date is 1 March. There will be another laptop sale on 1 September. Andreea sets a reminder to buy the laptop in the next sale. How many days does she have to wait to buy the laptop?

days

Negotiating prices involves a conversation between the customer and the seller to agree a price for a product or service. Negotiating often occurs at markets where prices might be flexible. In a negotiation, the customer usually tries to pay less than the advertised price. The seller has often already decided a minimum price that they will accept.

2 Andreea finds a bicycle and a watch at a market stall. The bicycle is priced at $150. She offers the seller $120. The seller says that they will accept a price halfway between $150 and $120.

The watch is priced at $80. Andreea offers the seller $50. Again, the seller says that they will accept a price halfway between $80 and $50. Andreea and the seller agree on both final prices.

How much does Andreea pay for:

a the bicycle? $

b the watch? $

c Which negotiation, the bicycle or the watch, gives Andreea the best percentage discount?

Some stores allow customers to pay for items in instalments. This means that the customer pays the money in equal amounts at equal time intervals, over a fixed period of time. This allows the customer to purchase expensive items without having to pay the full amount immediately.

3 Andreea is buying a new sofa. She looks at the option of paying for the sofa in instalments.

a Andreea finds a sofa that she likes that costs \$1500. She decides to pay a 25% deposit and then to pay for the remaining amount in equal monthly instalments over 18 months.

i How much does Andreea pay for the deposit?

\$

ii How much does she pay each month?

\$

b If Andreea paid a 30% deposit, what would her new monthly instalments be over 18 months? Give your answer to the nearest cent.

\$

When you buy in bulk, you buy larger quantities of items at one time. This often results in you paying less for each item than if you bought the item individually.

4 Andreea has to buy notebooks for her children for the next school year.

a Andreea finds a store that sells notebooks for \$2.25 each. The store also offers a bulk deal of 10 notebooks for \$18.90.

i How much would she pay for 10 notebooks if she bought them individually?

\$

ii How much does Andreea save per notebook by buying 10 notebooks in bulk?

\$

b The store buys the notebooks at a **cost price** of \$0.90 per notebook. How much profit do they earn, per notebook, for selling the notebooks at:

i the original retail price of \$2.25 each

\$

ii the bulk price of 10 notebooks for \$18.90?

\$

Ways to spend less continued

1 Aarav wants to buy a new pair of headphones. He finds two pairs of headphones that he likes. One is a basic pair of headphones that costs $15. Aarav thinks that this basic pair will be fine for occasional use. The other is a high-quality pair of headphones for $60. This pair would be ideal for daily use because of better sound quality and comfort.

a Aarav estimates that he will use the basic headphones approximately 50 times before they need to be replaced. What is the cost per use of the basic headphones?

$ ☐

b Aarav estimates that he will use the high-quality headphones approximately 500 times before they need to be replaced. What is the cost per use for the high-quality headphones?

$ ☐

c Which headphones would you advise Aarav to buy? Discuss with a partner.

2 Aarav needs a new pair of shoes for his school activities. He is trying to decide whether to buy a cheaper pair of shoes or a high-quality pair of shoes. The cheaper pair of shoes costs $30. Aarav estimates that this pair will last for 6 months. The high-quality pair of shoes costs $75. Aarav estimates that this pair will last for at least 18 months.

a If Aarav buys the cheaper pair of shoes, how much would he spend on shoes over 18 months, assuming that he buys a new pair every 6 months?

$ ☐

b If Aarav buys the high-quality pair of shoes, expected to last for the entire 18 months, how much more or less would he spend over the same period compared to if he bought the cheaper shoes?

$ ☐

c Which should Aarav buy? Discuss with a partner.

Sometimes buying in advance can help you to save money. For example, flights are often cheaper if you buy them a long time before your planned travel date.

3 Hana is planning to buy some plane tickets for a holiday.

a Hana checks the price of a flight to Paris four months before her holiday. She finds a ticket for $600. She decides to wait and check the price again two months before her holiday. The price of the same flight has increased to $900. By what percentage has the price increased?

☐ %

b Hana finds another flight. This flight costs $750 if she buys it two months before her holiday. This ticket would usually cost $1000 if bought on the day of travel. How much would she save, as a percentage, by booking this flight two months in advance?

[ ] %

c Discuss the following questions with a partner.

- *Why do you think airlines offer lower prices in advance?*
- *Can you name three more examples of purchases that are often cheaper if you buy them in advance?*

Sometimes, buying last minute can also help you to save money. You might see this with travel companies selling last minute tickets at a lower price and with cafés selling food items at a lower price just before their closing time.

4 **a** Carlos discovers that his favourite clothing store is stopping trading. They are having a sale with 60% off all items in their final week of trading. Carlos buys these four items from the store in the sale. The original prices are shown.

What is the price of each item after the discount has been applied?

Jeans	**T-shirt**
Sneakers	**Hat**

b After buying his clothes, Carlos goes to his local café. He arrives at the café an hour before closing time and finds that they have reduced the price of all the food items by 20%. Carlos buys a muffin, a cookie and a sandwich for $17, in total, after the 20% discount has been applied. What was the original total cost of these items?

$ [ ]

c Later that evening, Carlos uses a booking app on his phone to look for a coach ticket for the next day. There are a few last-minute tickets available. He buys a discounted ticket for $14. The original price for this ticket was $40. What was the discount on the ticket, as a percentage?

[ ] %

6 Financial responsibility

Paying bills

Households pay utility bills for essential services such as electricity, water and gas. These bills are usually charged monthly or **quarterly**, depending on the billing cycle set by the utility provider.

1 Henry moved into a new apartment three months ago. He has just received his first quarterly bill. He is trying to work out how much he has been paying for electricity over the past three months. His electricity provider charges him \$0.15 per kilowatt hour (kWh). In the first three months, he used the following amounts of electricity:

January 350 kWh *February 420 kWh* *March 290 kWh*

a How much did Henry pay for electricity in:

i January **ii** February **iii** March **iv** the three months in total?

January \$ ______ February \$ ______

March \$ ______ Total \$ ______

Average electricity used per month = total electricity used/number of months

b How many kWh of electricity did Henry use, on average, per month in this **quarter**?

Give your answer to two decimal places.

c How much money did Henry spend on electricity, on average, per month in this quarter?

Subscriptions, such as for video streaming services, provide users with access to a specific service or content for a recurring fee. Users typically sign up for a subscription plan. This plan gives the user access to the service's content for a certain length of time. Sometimes, providers charge less per month if a customer subscribes for a longer length of time.

2 Henry has just signed up for a video streaming service.

a The video streaming service charges $12.25 per month. How much will Henry pay for the service over 6 months?

b After 6 months, Henry decides to change to a different video streaming service. This new service offers a discounted annual subscription for $130. In one year, how much less will Henry pay by using this annual subscription compared to using the monthly subscription?

$

c Another video streaming service charges $14.75 per month for a 12 month subscription, but new customers get 50% off the first 6 months. In one year, how much more or less would Henry pay by using this subscription compared to the subscription in part **b**?

When renting property, a tenant pays a regular fee to the **landlord** to live in the property. The rental fee is usually paid monthly.

3 **a** The rental fee for the apartment Henry lives in is $815 per month. How much will Henry pay in rental fees for 6 months?

b After living in the apartment for 6 months, Henry's landlord increases the rent to $850 per month. Henry decides to find a roommate to split the rental fees. If they share the $850 rental fees equally, how much will Henry and his roommate each pay, per month?

c Some landlords charge a rental fee, and then the tenant is responsible for paying their own utilities. Some landlords charge a rental fee that also includes utilities.

Which option do you think is better for a landlord or for a tenant?

Discuss some of the advantages and disadvantages of both options with a partner.

Your first mobile phone

Your first mobile phone will be one of your first financial responsibilities. It is important to consider the cost of buying the phone, the monthly bills, and any additional expenses such as accessories or insurance. There are lots of different types of phones and different ways to pay for them, for example, 'pay as you go', or a contract.

1 Harry goes to the mobile phone store to buy his first phone. He sees the following three phones:

Premium smartphone	Budget smartphone	Non-smartphone device
Cost $1000 This phone has a powerful camera and a large touchscreen.	**Cost $500** This phone has a basic camera and a small touchscreen.	**Cost $50** This phone does not have a touchscreen.

Which of the phones should Harry choose?

Think about the price and the features of each phone.

Discuss the advantages and disadvantages of each phone with a partner.

When you buy a phone on pay as you go, you top up your phone account with money. You then use the money to pay for services such as calls, texts or internet usage.

2 Harry buys a pay as you go phone. He buys $15 of top up for his new phone. Text messages cost 12c each to send and calls cost 3c per minute. Internet usage is included in the package price.

a In the first weekend of using his phone, Harry makes 3.5 hours of calls and sends 37 text messages. How much money does he have left on his phone?

b Harry uses all of the money on his phone so he buys another $15 of top up. During the next week, he only sends text messages. He does not make any phone calls. At the end of the week, he has $6.12 left on his phone. How many text messages did he send this week?

c Harry uses all of the money on his phone again so he buys another $35 top up. During the next week, he makes only phone calls. He does not send any text messages. At the end of the week he has $28.28 left on his phone. What was the total duration of his phone calls this week?

When you buy a phone on contract you pay for the device and services for a fixed period of time – usually 12, 24 or 36 months. You pay a contract fee each month. The total cost of a phone contract usually costs more than you would pay to buy the phone. However, phones can be expensive, so paying monthly is a good way to spread the cost.

3 **a** Meghan wants to buy a new phone. She sees a smartphone on a 12 month contract. The contract costs $25.99 per month. How much would Meghan pay for this contract, in total?

b Meghan sees a special offer that gives new customers 50% off for the first four months of the same contract as in part **a**. How much would the 12 month contract now cost, in total?

With a SIM-only phone contract, you buy a SIM card with a set amount of minutes, text messages and data over a specific period of time. You buy the phone separately.

4 **a** Archie is shopping online and considering three SIM-only contract plans:

Plan A	Plan B	Plan C
1000 minutes, 5000 text messages and 10GB data for $20.99 per month, 12 months	800 minutes, 6000 text messages and 8GB data for $18.99 per month, 24 months	1200 minutes, 4000 text messages and 12GB data for $22.99 per month, 26 months

Which plan offers the best value for money in terms of minutes?

b On the same website, Archie sees a 24 month contract plan for $40.99 a month. This contract gives the same benefits as SIM-only plan A, but it also includes a phone. He would prefer the SIM-only plan, and save money on the contract by buying a phone separately. What is the maximum the phone can cost for Archie to save money?

$

5 With a partner, discuss the advantages and disadvantages of pay as you go, a contract with the phone included, and buying a SIM-only phone contract. Which option would you prefer?

Your first bank account

Current accounts are bank accounts that allow individuals to manage their day-to-day finances. These accounts typically offer services such as depositing and withdrawing money, making purchases using a debit card, and paying bills.

1 Femi has just opened his first current account. The **opening balance** is $0.

a Femi deposits $100.50 into his account. He then withdraws $40.25 to buy a computer game. He also uses the debit card linked to the account to pay $30.75 to go to the movies. How much money does Femi have left?

b In the second month, Femi deposits four weekly allowances of $20.75. He also withdraws $15.50 from his account each of the four weeks to pay for his lunch. If these are the only transactions he makes, how much money does Femi have in his account at the end of the second month?

The opening balance in the second month is the same as the **closing balance** in the first month.

c Femi's current account has a monthly fee of $5.25. How much does Femi pay in fees, in total, each year?

Savings accounts are for saving money rather than for frequent transactions. The money deposited in a savings account remains there until the account holder withdraws it.

2 Femi's older brother, Fisayo, has just opened a savings account with an opening balance of $150.

Remember to include Fisayo's opening deposit.

a Fisayo earns $2200 a month. He deposits 10% of his earnings into his savings account every month. How much money does Fisayo have in his account after one year?

b In the second year, Fisayo decides to deposit 15% of his monthly earnings into his savings account. How much money will he have in his account after two years?

c In the third year, Fisayo continues to deposit 15% of his monthly earnings into his savings account. However, he misses two monthly deposits. How much does Fisayo have in his savings account, in total, after three years?

A **joint account** is a bank account shared by two or more individuals. They are typically used by couples, family members, or business partners. Each account holder has equal access to the account. Joint accounts are often used for managing shared expenses, such as household bills or business funds.

3 Femi's parents have just opened a joint account with an opening balance of $500.

a In the first month of using the joint account, Femi's parents deposit another $500 into the account. They withdraw $150 to spend on groceries, $140 to spend on dining out and $50 to spend on entertainment. How much money is left in their joint account?

b In the second month, Femi's father's salary of $1500 is deposited into the account. Femi's Mum's salary of $2000 is also deposited into the account. $1200 for rent, $300 for utility bills and $220 for transportation costs are all paid out of the account. Additionally, Femi's parents withdraw $200 for personal spending. How much money is left in their joint account now?

Understanding your pay statement

A **pay statement** (also known as a **salary statement**) shows an employee's salary and any deductions for a specific time period. Gross pay is the total amount of money an employee earns before any deductions are subtracted, such as taxes, insurance, or retirement contributions. Take-home pay (net pay) is the amount of money an employee actually receives after all deductions have been subtracted from the gross pay.

Pay Statement

Employee Name:	Alessandro Rossi
Employee ID:	123456
Department:	Humanities
Position:	Lecturer
Payment Details:	
Salary Period:	December 2024
Payment Date:	19th
Salary Amount:	$2700.00
Earnings:	
Gross Salary:	$2700.00
Deductions:	
Federal Income Tax:	-$250.00
State Income Tax:	-$100.00
Social Security Tax (FICA):	-$150.00
Medical insurance	-$50.00
Net Pay:	
Total Deductions:	-$550.00
Net Salary:	$2150.00

1 Alessandro has just received his first pay statement after his first month at his new job.

a Use the information on the pay statement to answer the following questions.

i How much is Alessandro's monthly gross salary?

$ ______

ii What is his monthly net salary?

$ ______

iii How much does Alessandro pay monthly for social security tax?

$ ______

iv What is Alessandro's lowest monthly deduction?

______

b How much are Alessandro's deductions, in total, per year?

______

c What is Alessandro's annual net salary?

______

Pay statements usually also show retirement savings. Retirement savings are a portion of an employee's earnings that are set aside for their retirement. This is usually done through a retirement savings plan, where a certain percentage of the employee's gross pay is contributed to a retirement fund. The contributions are deducted before taxes are calculated.

2 Elena has just received her first pay statement. She is working out her retirement contributions.

a Elena's employer offers a retirement savings plan as follows:

If she contributes 10% of her gross pay into her retirement savings, her employer will contribute an additional 5% of her gross pay.

Elena's monthly gross pay is $800. What will be the total monthly contributions into her retirement savings?

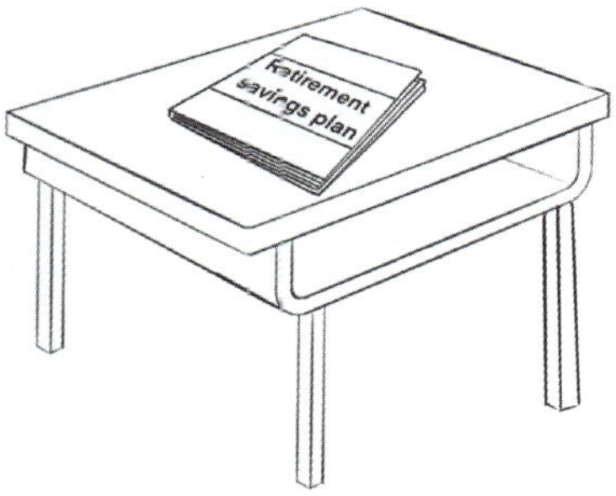

$ [ ]

b If Elena increases/decreases her contributions, her employer will also increase/decrease their contributions in the same proportion. Fill in the missing values in this table.

Elena's contributions (% of her gross salary)	Elena's contributions ($)	Employer's contributions (% of Elena's gross salary)	Employer's contributions ($)
5%			
10%		5%	
15%			
		10%	

c Why do you think it is important to save for a retirement fund? Discuss with a partner.

In many countries, individuals pay tax on their earnings. Tax codes on a pay statement show how much of an individual's income is **taxable**. The tax code is based on their income, tax allowances, and other factors.

3 a Dion has just received his pay statement. His tax code is A. This means he has a tax-free personal allowance of $12 600 for the tax year. He then pays 30% tax on earnings over $12 600. If Dion earns $1300 in a month, how much tax will he pay for that month?

b Dion receives a bonus of $500 in addition to his regular monthly income. How does this affect the amount of tax Dion will pay for the month, assuming his tax code remains the same?

c Dion's tax code is adjusted to B in the new tax year. This reduces his tax-free personal allowance to $11 000. He then still pays 30% tax on earnings over $11 000. If Dion earns £1500 in a month under the new tax code, how much tax will he pay for that month?

Checking bills and receipts

1 Mrs Johnson goes to the supermarket to buy some groceries. She pays for her shopping with a $20 note and is given $4.80 in change. She thinks she has received the wrong change but is not sure.

Here is a list of the items Mrs Johnson buys:

- *Houseplant - $2.60*
- *Juice – 50c*
- *Apples – 75c*
- *Bin bags - $3.00*
- *Hand soap - $2.00*
- *Instant coffee - $5.40*
- *Olive oil - $2.30*
- ***Amount given - $20***

Has Mrs Johnson been given the correct change? If not, how much change should she have received?

It can sometimes be useful to estimate the total cost of, for example, a shopping trip or a meal at a restaurant. This will help you to notice if the bill is incorrect.

2 The Johnson family go to a restaurant. They order three main courses, costing $21.95, $15.50 and $17.25, and four drinks, costing $7.40, $3.75, $3.75 and $9.50.

a Using a rounding method, estimate the total cost of their food and drink.

b Calculate the exact total cost of their food and drink.

c The restaurant automatically adds a 20% tip to every bill. Use your estimate from part **a** to estimate how much money is added as a tip.

d Calculate the exact value of the tip.

3 The Johnson household are charged for electricity and gas at two different daily rates.

Electricity costs $1.55 per day.
Gas costs 75c per day.

Over the course of a 30-day month, the family uses the electricity each day. During this month, they stop using the gas for 15 days because the weather is hot during this time.

For this month, how much was the family's:

a electricity bill

b gas bill

c total bill?

Fill in the blanks in the utility bill below with the correct amounts.

UTILITY BILL

Electricity $1.55/day ____________

Gas 75c/day ____________

Total ($) ____________

4 The Johnson family also pay a property tax each month. Their total monthly bills are $540.30 and the property tax is 18% of their total bills.

a Using a rounding method, estimate how much the Johnson family pay each month for property tax.

b Calculate how much property tax the Johnson family pay exactly each month. Give your answer to the nearest cent.

c Do you ever use estimates to get an idea of how much you will pay for things? Discuss with a partner.

Checking bank statements

A **bank statement** lists all the money that has been paid into the bank account, along with the date this money was paid in and who paid the money in.

1 a Mildred's opening bank balance at the start of May is $528.74. Her bank statement for May shows the following money paid into her account:

Mildred Jones
01 May 2025 to 31 May 2025

CENTRAL BANK

Date	Payment type	Details	Out ($)	In ($)	Balance ($)
					$528.74
02 May	Online	Office Staff Ltd		$327.44	
14 May	Cash	Mrs G Jones		$50.00	
20 May	Online	Cool Clothes Ltd		$20.82	

What is the total amount paid into Mildred's account in May?

b Mildred's bank statement for June shows the following money paid into her account:

Mildred Jones
01 June 2025 to 30 June 2025

CENTRAL BANK

Date	Payment type	Details	Out ($)	In ($)	Balance ($)
02 June	Online	Office Staff Ltd		$352.34	
19 June	Cash	Mr A Jones		$32.00	
24 June	Online	Miss S Mehra		$10.25	

i Using the information from part **a**, fill in the opening balance on the June bank statement.

ii What is the total amount paid into Mildred's account for June?

c Why do you think bank statements include the date and source of each amount paid into an account? Discuss with a partner.

Bank statements also list the money that has been paid out of the bank account, the date the money was paid out and who the money was paid to.

2 In July, Mildred withdraws money from her account to make the following ten different purchases:

$124.11 for groceries

$30.23 for dinner at a restaurant

$20.53 for movie tickets

$40.79 for clothes

$25.31 for a birthday gift

$35.47 for transportation expenses

$15.61 for university supplies

$45.83 for a phone bill

$60.37 for a video game

$55.97 for a gym membership

Mildred wants to categorize these purchases into the following five categories:

	Food and groceries	Entertainment	Personal items	Utilities and bills	Recreation and hobbies
Total ($)					

a Write each of the above payments in the correct category in the table.

b How much did Mildred spend, in total, for each category in July? Write the totals in the table.

The **balance** on a bank statement shows the total amount of money in the bank account at a specific time.

3 Here is Mildred's bank statement for August:

Mildred Jones
01 August 2025 to 31 August 2025

CENTRAL BANK

Date	Payment type	Details	Out ($)	In ($)	Balance ($)
					$509.63
02 Aug	Online	Office staff Ltd		$2500.00	
03 Aug	Online	Rent payment	$1000.00		
05 Aug	Debit card	Food Store	$150.23		
07 Aug	Debit card	Grant's Garage	$40.56		
10 Aug	Online	Internet payment	$55.80		
15 Aug	Debit card	Spice Garden Curry House	$75.30		
20 Aug	Online	Electricity payment	$90.47		
25 Aug	Online	Phone bill	$65.70		
28 Aug	Debit card	Best Clothes Ltd	$120.00		
31 Aug	Cash	Mrs G Jones		$150.00	

What is Mildred's closing balance at the end of August?

$ ______

Glossary

50/30/20 principle a principle that says that when you earn money you should spend 50% of the money on your 'needs', spend 30% of the money on your 'wants' and save 20% of your money

acquisition when one company buys another company to increase the size of the original company

allowance money that is given to someone, usually weekly or monthly; a form of pocket money. In tax, an allowance is the amount of income an individual can earn before they need to start paying tax

annually every year

annual salary the total amount of salary a person earns in one year

asset a thing of value, that a person or company owns

ATM (automatic teller machine) a machine that can be used for taking money out of a bank account, using a bank card and a PIN number

balance the amount of money left in an account when all transactions have been made, often calculated at the end of each month

bank account an arrangement with a bank; a way of managing your own money by paying money into the bank to keep it safe, and taking out money when it is needed

bank statement a monthly summary from a bank that gives details of all money paid in and all money taken out of the account with dates of all transactions

bill a document that shows how much you owe somebody for goods or services, for example, electricity or gas bills

budget *(noun)* the amount of money that a person has to spend on something

budget *(verb)* to track and plan your spending and saving

bulk a large number of items

bureau de change a place where you can exchange one currency for another

business expenses all the money that a business spends to operate

business profit the money a business makes after subtracting all their business expenses from their revenue

career a job, for which people train for, and stay in for a long time

career path the series of jobs or roles that a person does as part of their career

change the amount of money received back from a seller/lender when you have paid too much money

charity an organization that helps people or animals in need

cheque a printed document that you can write on and sign as a way of paying for something instead of using money

chip and pin device a machine that uses a system of paying for something with a bank card, which has a microchip stored in it; the user then proves their identity by typing a personal identification number (PIN) into the machine

client a person who uses the services or advice of a professional person or organization

cost price the price that a retailer buys items for (from a wholesaler)

currencies the different types of money that different countries use

consumer a person who buys goods or services

coupon a voucher (or digital code) given out to customers which gives them a discount when buying goods or services

debit card a plastic card provided by your bank that is used to get money from your account out of a machine (ATM) or to pay for items using a chip and pin device or contactless payment

demand the desire or need of customers for goods or services

deposit ***(verb)*** to part-pay for something at the beginning of a transaction; the rest of the money is usually paid at a later date and often in instalments

discount a reduction in price

disposable income the amount of money someone has left after subtracting their bills and expenses from their income (usually worked out monthly)

diversification when investors buy shares in a wide range of companies, rather than investing in only one company, to decrease their risk of losing money

donate to give to charity

economy all the money in a place, such as a town, a city or a country, and the way that people in a place make money and spend money

emergency fund money that is put aside to pay for unexpected costs, such as repairing a car or damage to part of a house

employer a person, or company, that pays its staff a salary in return for doing work for them

employee a person who is employed by a company and who is paid a salary in return for doing work for the company

entrepreneur a person who makes money by starting or running businesses

environmental relating to the natural conditions in which people, animals and plants live

essential things that are needed, such as food and shelter

excess a fixed amount that someone has to pay when making an insurance claim

exchange rate the value of one currency, at a given time, for the purpose of exchanging it with another currency

expenditure all the money that is spent

expenses all the things you spend money on

fare the cost to travel on public transport

fee an amount of money paid, usually for a service

financial advisor a person who provides help and advice to an individual or business regarding saving and spending money, investments, mortgages, and so on

fixed expenses costs that need to be paid monthly or annually that are the same amount each month/year, for example, a fixed monthly contract for a mobile phone

freelance earn money by selling your own work or services to several different organizations rather than being employed by one particular organization

goods products; things that are made and sold

government the people who control the country; those who make the laws

gross salary the amount of money a person earns before deductions, such as tax, are applied

hourly rate a fixed amount of pay that someone earns for each hour that they work

income all the money that a person earns or receives

income tax an amount that an employee has to pay (to the government) out of their salary; this tax usually pays for amenities such as schools and hospitals

inflation the rise of prices of goods and services and the rise in salaries over time

instalment a payment that is made regularly, over a fixed period of time, until something has been fully paid for

insurance a payment that you make to a company and, in return, they agree to pay costs if you lose or damage something

insurance policy a document to prove the purchase of insurance for something, such as a car or a home. The policy will state all the terms and conditions of the contract with the insurer

investment bank a business that acts as a financial advisor for governments and companies. Investment banks can help with mergers and acquisitions of companies

investment broker a person who provides impartial investment advice

investors people who buy and sell assets, such as shares in companies, to make money

joint account a bank account shared by two or more people (for example, a married couple, or business partners)

landlord a property owner who allows people to live or work in their property in exchange for rent

lend when a bank or a family member gives money to someone temporarily, and then the person pays it back when they no longer need it

loan money that an organization such as a bank lends to someone, for example, to enable them to study, or to start a new business

loyalty scheme a way of rewarding customers for continually shopping at the same place – the customer may be offered discounts or free products after they have spent a certain amount of money

merger when two or more companies combine to form a larger company

mobile payment a payment made for goods or services using a mobile phone or smartwatch

mobile wallet an app on a mobile device that stores debit card details

monthly every month

mortgage an agreement made with a bank or similar organization, where the bank lends an individual, or couple, money specifically to buy a house. This is then paid back to the bank in instalments, over time

net pay the amount of money a person earns after deductions, such as tax, are applied

net worth the amount of money a company is valued at, based on all its assets

non-essential not needed, but may like to have, such as treats

online voucher code a digital code given out to customers which gives them a discount when buying goods or services when shopping online

opening balance the amount in a bank account when it is first opened, or at the beginning of a certain period

overtime additional hours worked that are not part of a person's basic contracted hours

pay rise an increase in pay/salary

pay statement also known as a salary statement or pay slip, shows an employee how much they are getting paid, including any deductions such as tax, pensions or charitable contributions

pocket money a regular amount of money that children are given, usually by their parents or grandparents

premium the amount paid to an insurance company each month, or annually, for an insurance policy

producer a person who makes goods or provides services

profit the money that an individual or business has left, after paying for all its costs

profitability how likely a business is to make a profit

promotion when a person moves to a higher position within a company where they work, which usually comes with a pay rise. Promotion is also used to describe a type of offer or discount that stores offer customers

quarter every three months of the year

quarterly four times a year / once every three months

quote a written record of how much something will cost to do, usually given out by tradespeople before it is agreed for them to do a job

receipt a piece of paper or an electronic document that shows that goods or services have been paid for, and how much was paid

reduced decreased in price

renovate make improvements to something (for example, property) in order to increase its value

rent the money paid to a landlord (property owner) by a tenant, to live at their property

repay to give money back to a bank or other lender

retirement savings an amount deducted from a person's gross salary which is invested on their behalf until they retire, when it is paid back to them

revenue all the money an individual or company receives from selling goods and services (before any deductions)

salary money that people earn by doing a job, usually paid monthly by an employer

salary statement also known as a pay statement or pay slip, shows an employee how much they are getting paid, including any deductions such as tax, pensions or charitable contributions

savings the total money that someone has saved up

savings account a type of bank account, used for when money is kept in the account for a long time, where the account holder earns interest on the money that is in the account

second hand not new, has been owned by someone else before

self-employed not employed by a company – instead, working for yourself and doing work for different clients to make money

services things that people do, or provide, for other people, that can be bought and sold, for example, fixing a leaking tap, cutting someone's hair

socially responsible investment an investment made in a socially and environmentally responsible company

stock market a trading place where people buy and sell shares in companies

supply the amount of something that is currently available to be used

tax/taxes money that an individual has to pay to the government, used to pay for public services; tax is paid on income (by individuals) or on profits (by businesses); tax is also often paid on goods and services

taxable describes the money that you have to pay tax on

tax rate the percentage of tax taken from a person's salary as income tax; this rate increases as the salary increases

tenant a person who lives in a rented property and pays rent to the landlord (the property owner)

tip money given, at the discretion of the customer, to service workers for doing a good job

trade when people exchange goods and services with each other

unit of account a standard numerical monetary unit of measurement, used to denote the value of goods, services, and other transactions

value for money how much of something you get, or how good something is, compared to how much it costs

variable expenses costs that are different each month/year, for example, transport costs, or grocery costs will vary each month

weekly every week

withdraw to take money out of a bank account

withdrawal a transaction of taking money our of a bank account

worth valued at